DOONESBURY

By Garry Trudeau

Foreword By Erich Segal

Andrews and McMeel, Inc.—Kansas City

A Universal Press Syndicate Company

Copyright © 1971 by G. B. Trudeau
Published by American Heritage Press
a subsidiary of McGraw-Hill, Inc.
Published in Canada by McGraw-Hill Company
of Canada, Ltd.
This paperback edition is published by
Alligator Books, a division of Andrews and
McMeel, Inc. Doonesbury is syndicated
internationally by Universal Press Syndicate,
6700 Squibb Road, Mission, Ks. 66202.
First printing, March, 1973
Second printing, December, 1973
Third printing, April, 1974
Fourth printing, December, 1974
Fifth printing, October, 1975
Sixth printing, September, 1976
Seventh printing, March, 1979
Library of Congress Catalog Card Number: 73-9100

ISBN 0-8362-0550-2
Design by Calligraph, New Haven, Ct.

To Annie,
who only likes a few of them

Foreword

by Erich Segal

There is an ulterior motive to my writing these words for the initial volume of the *Compleat Workes of Garry Trudeau*. Simply stated, I would like the world to know that Garry was once a student of mine at Yale. This might suggest that I am in some way responsible for Trudeau's comic genius and thereby attract the interest of future biographers, thesis writers, and (hopefully) groupies.

Now there is a certain truth in my statement.

Garry Trudeau actually did take my course.

But that's all. As far as who taught whom, it's quite another matter. *I* learned from Garry.

What I know about campus sex, drugs, radicals, and crazies I learned from Garry Trudeau.

I also know that if the previous sentence is ever quoted out of context I may be out of a job. But the truth must be served.

Of course you readers understood at once that I got my education from Garry's *cartoons*. Right? I think it was Voltaire who said that comedy provided the best of all possible mirrors to the life it mocked. Anyway, it bears repeating: we discover today's college young in Trudeau's mirror.

Moreover, Trudeau sees the campus and its divers denizens as people —not merely raw material for comic distortion. His technique is not gross hyperbole, but graceful epitome. He reduces life to its essential foibles. We laugh because what he shows us is so true, but more important, we smile because he has been so gentle. We are grateful that he prefers wisecracks to slapstick. We wouldn't want anyone to get hurt— especially us. For we are his subjects, as are all the funny little fragile people—even the football players.

One of the most common put-downs of today's young people is that they lack a sense of humor. Humbug. Garry Trudeau is an original comic talent who can bring smiles to both overbearing parents and ungrateful kids. He is neither Disney nor Feiffer; he is uniquely himself. Which, by the way, is the definition of a real artist.

And remember, I said it first.

Ezra Stiles College
Yale University
November, 1970

DESPITE PREVIOUS FAILURES AT THIS MIXER TONITE, MIKE "THE MIX," INEXPERIENCED BUT EAGER FRESHMAN, STILL LOOKS AROUND FOR HIS FIRST SCORE OF THE EVENING.
SPOTTING A YOUNG LOVELY, HE APPROACHES HER..
HI THERE! HOW ABOUT A LITTLE DANCE?
SURE, YOU GROSS SKINNY LITTLE FROSH!
HA HA HA HA HA
IF I WEREN'T SO SKINNY AND LITTLE, I'D RAPE HER FOR THAT.
AH HA HA HA HA
G B Trudeau

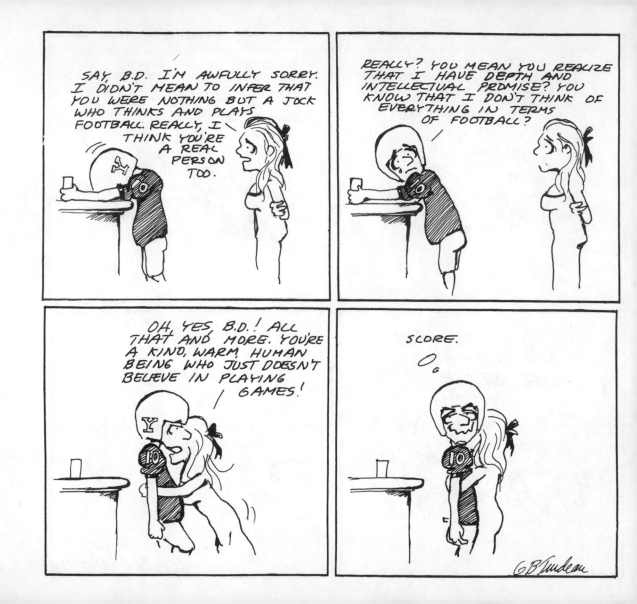

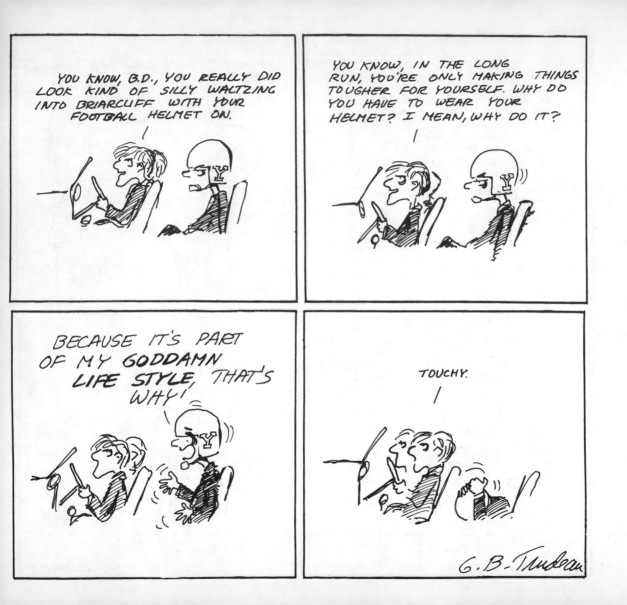

ALTHOUGH THE KING HAS DROPPED ROTC, GIVEN THE GYM TO THE CITY OF NEW HAVEN, AND HAS CONSENTED TO TURN HIS HOUSE INTO A GIRL'S DORM, "MEGAPHONE" MARK FINDS COMPROMISE DISTASTEFUL.. HE DECIDES TO TAKE DRASTIC ACTION...
O.K. EVERYBODY, NOW LET'S GET SERIOUS! I GAVE YOU YOUR CHANCE! SO GUESS WHAT NOW...
WE'RE TAKING OVER THIS OFFICE! HOW ABOUT THAT, HUH?
OH, YEAH, WELL ALRIGHTY. LET ME JUST GET TOGETHER HERE A FEW OF MY PERSONAL EFFECTS...
BEFORE I GO, SHALL I SHOW YOU WHERE I KEEP MY SHERRY AND CIGARS?..
GB Trudeau

WHAT?... WELL, ACTUALLY I THINK I WAS MORE THAN FAIR WITH THE PRESIDENT. HE MOVED OVER TO STAY AT THE TAFT AND I MOVED IN HERE IN AN ORDERLY FASHION...
... BUT LET ME ADD THAT YESTERDAY WHILE I WAS QUIETLY XEROXING HIS PRIVATE FILES, 25 CAMPUS COPS WITH NIGHT CLUBS JUST BURST IN THE ROOM WITHOUT WARNING! ...
THEY FLAILED AT ME MERCILESSLY! "OH GOD, STOP, PLEASE, STOP!" I PLEADED, WHILE BLOOD SPURTED DOWN MY FOREHEAD, "PLEASE STOP!"
BUT THEY BEAT ME SENSELESS! SENSELESS, I TELL YOU!
PRACTICING UP FOR MY FIRST PRESS CONFERENCE.
G B Trudeau

HAVING SPOTTED THE FUZ OUTSIDE THE HOUSE, "MEGAPHONE" MARK IS UNDERSTANDABLY NERVOUS WHEN HE HEARS A KNOCK ON THE DOOR..
KNOCK! KNOCK!
EXCUSE ME, ARE YOU "MEGAPHONE" MARK?
YUP. UH-HUH.
PSST...
WHAT A GAS. HEH-HEH. GET IT?
GBTrudeau

WELL, SATURDAY NIGHT ONCE AGAIN AND SO I AND MY FRIENDS HAVE LEFT SCHOOL AND HAVE JUST NOW ARRIVED AT A NEARBY WOMEN'S COLLEGE DANCE! OH WOW! EXCITEMENT PLUS!
I CAREFULLY SCRUTINIZE THE GIRLS. I AM EAGER BUT WARY BECAUSE OF THE ANCIENT NOTION THAT THE GIRLS HERE AT SMITH COLLEGE ARE PARTIAL TO EMOTIONAL COMMITMENT... ...AH, A LOVELY APPROACHETH..
HI, THERE. MY NAME'S DORIS. DO YOU THINK YOU COULD LEARN TO LOVE ME?
I WONDER IF THE GUYS ARE READY TO GO YET...
GBTrudeau

NOW SEE HERE, DORIS, I'M NOT UP FOR ANY INVOLVEMENT! I JUST CAME TO THIS SMITH MIXER TO HAVE A GOOD TIME, UNDERSTAND?
SOB
OH, UNSPEAKABLE SORROW... I THOUGHT THAT YOU COULD LOVE ME, MIKE, AND THAT YOU WOULD LOVE ME. BUT YOU DON'T, AND THAT BEING THE CASE, I JUST WOULDN'T FEEL RIGHT ABOUT GOING TO BED WITH YOU.
YOU KNOW, DORIS, PERHAPS I'M BEING A LITTLE HASTY...
GBTrudeau

WELL, HERE WE ARE, DRIVING BACK FROM ANOTHER DISASTROUS MIXER. OH, MY EGO CRIES OUT FROM THE BEATING IT HAS TAKEN...
2-17
OH, BOY, DO I HATE MIXERS! IT'S AMAZING HOW MUCH! JUST TONITE I TOLD THAT TO MY ROOMMATE SCOT AS WE DROVE UP TO THIS MIXER..
I GUESS IT WAS LESS THAN THREE HOURS AGO WHEN AS WE WERE DRIVING ALONG, I TOLD SCOT, "BOY DO I HATE MIXERS." MY ROOMMATE SCOT SAID BACK TO ME, "MIKE, WHAT YOU GET OUT OF A MIXER DEPENDS ON WHAT YOU PUT INTO IT."
I HATE MY ROOMMATE SCOT.
G B Trudeau

I HAVE AN ANNOUNCEMENT TO MAKE!
THAT LAST PLAY I GOT MY PANTS DIRTY! WHY? I GOT MY PANTS DIRTY BECAUSE OUR LEFT TACKLE LET THROUGH HIS MAN WHOM I SUBSEQUENTLY HAD TO SHAKE OFF!!
ACTUALLY I HAVE TO ADMIRE THE SPIRIT BEHIND THAT.
G B Trudeau

O.K., BULLDOGS, NEXT PLAY IS AN END SWEEP. FRANK, YOU TAKE THE ROLLOUT. O.K., GOT IT?
EXCUSE, ME, B.D.
YES, WILLIAM?
B.D., WHILE I APPLAUD YOUR DECISION OF AN END SWEEP, I QUESTION YOUR CHOICE OF FRANK AS THE MAN TO RUN. ALTHOUGH HE IS FLEXIBLE AND ALERT, I WOULD SAY THAT THE CAPABILITIES OF JONATHON ARE MORE SUITABLE FOR THIS THIRD DOWN SITUATION.
I'M AFRAID I WOULD HAVE TO DISAGREE, WILLIAM. JONATHON'S TEMPERAMENT HAS BEEN TEMPERED BY AN EARLY EXPOSURE TO A LOW ACHIEVEMENT ORIENTED UPBRINGING.
YES, I AGREE.
I ALSO DON'T FEEL AS IF I SHOULD RUN, NOW, WILLY. CAN YOU UNDERSTAND THAT?
I APPRECIATE YOUR HONESTY JONATHON. O.K. B.D., LET FRANK RUN.
BEST T-GROUP IN THE LEAGUE.
G B Trudeau

2-27
SO THIS IS YOUR ROOM, EH, MIKE MY BOY...
OH GOD, I CAN'T BELIEVE I'VE ASKED THIS GIRL. I'VE GOT TO THINK OF SOME WAY TO MAKE HER WANT TO LEAVE... SHOCK HER, GROSS HER OUT.
ALRIGHT, NOW LISTEN UP! I COULDN'T GET A HOTEL ROOM FOR YOU, SO YOU'RE GOING TO HAVE TO SHARE MY BED WITH ME! HOW ABOUT THAT, HUH?!
OH, GRRR... YOU SEXY BASTARD, I'LL DO IT.
I WONDER IF SHE TAKES THE BOOTS OFF WHEN SHE SLEEPS
G.B.Trudeau

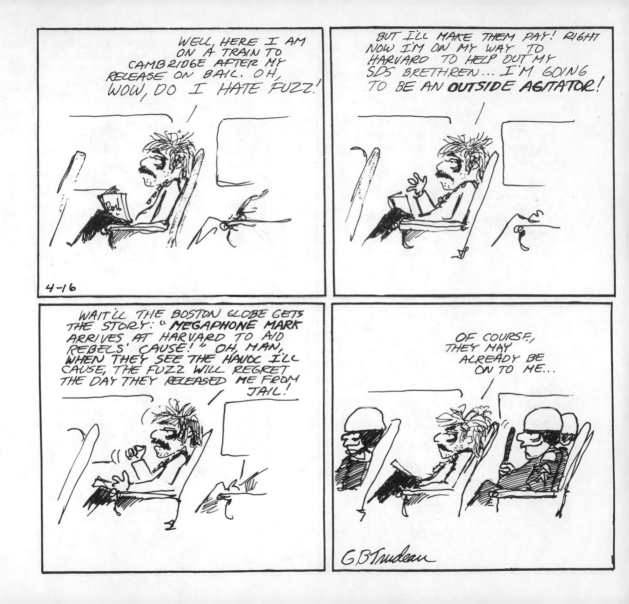

IT'S ANOTHER AFTERNOON AT THE ADMISSIONS OFFICE, AS ALAN THE AMAZING ADMISSIONS OFFICER CONTINUES WITH HIS CONTROVERSIAL NEW SCREENING PROCESS THAT ALLOWS US TO ACCEPT OR REJECT BORDERLINE CASES..
4-7
AH, MRS. WASSERMAN... IF THE NEXT CANDIDATE IS READY, COULD YOU PLEASE SEND HER IN.
HI! I WANT TO COME TO YALE.
ACCEPT.
GBTrudeau

O.K., NOW COMES THE PAYOFF PLAY!! I CALL IT THE "OHIO EXPRESS." THE FRONT LINE THROWS UP A GOOD BLOCK. I FADE BACK TO OUR OWN 5 YARD LINE.
WAITING UNTIL AT LEAST THREE MEN ARE UPON ME, BALANCING ON ONE FOOT, I THROW AN UNDERHAND 95 YARD SPIRAL WHICH I'LL RUN DOWN AND CATCH ON THE GOAL LINE. O.K. BREAK!!
RIGHT.
G. B. Trudeau

O.K. WHO'S INTERESTED IN TAKING THE BALL THIS PLAY?
ME!!
NO, NO! I WANNA, I WANNA!
NO, LEMME! I WANNA TAKE IT!
AW, COME ON I ASKED FIRST.
NO FAIR! NO FAIR! I GOT FIRST DIBS!
LISTEN, YOU BETTER GIMME THE BALL OR I'LL KNOCK YOUR HEAD OFF!
LIAR, LIAR, PANTS ON FIRE!
YEAH!
OH YEAH, TOUGH GUY?
O.K. LET THE SISSY HAVE IT, BUT I'LL SEE YOU LATER, BUDDY!
BENEATH THE COOL EXTERIOR OF A FOOTBALL HUDDLE LURK THE SUBTLE DYNAMICS OF A NURSERY SCHOOL RECESS.
GBTrudeau

O.K. WHAT'S ALL THIS I HEAR ABOUT A NEW PLAY YOU GUYS HAVE WORKED OUT FOR HARVARD?
WELL, B.D., ACTUALLY IT'S A SPECIAL TWO-PART PLAY- IT STARTS OFF WITH WHAT WE CALL THE "GATTO OUT," WHEREIN TWO SAFETYS PINCER IN ON THE END, SMASH THE DEFENDING BACKS AND RIP GATTO'S HEAD OFF...
LOVE IT!!
YEA!
BOOLA, BOOLA!
...THEN THE SECOND PART OF THIS PLAY IS THE "HORNBLOWER HACK," IN WHICH THE ENTIRE FRONT LINE FORMS A PHALANX WHICH DRIVES IN OFF LEFT TACKLE, AND PROCEEDS TO MAIM AND RIP HORNBLOWER TO SHREDS!
MAUL!
OH YES!
KILL!!
I LIKE IT, I LIKE IT.
GB Trudeau

IT'S ANOTHER LONELY NIGHT FOR LONESOME LINDA LOCAL, PERT ELEVENTH-GRADER AT DAY PROSPECT, AS SHE CRUISES THROUGH THE OLD CAMPUS AREA LOOKING FOR A NICE YALE MALE WHO WILL TREAT HER KIND...
4-9
DESPITE HER NEAT NEW BLACK PEA JACKET AND JAZZY BELLBOTTOM JEANS, THE FELLAS ARE PASSING LONESOME LINDA BY, NOT REALIZING THAT SHE TOO IS A WARM HUMAN BEING.
THERE GOES ANOTHER ONE.. I GUESS I MIGHT AS WELL FACE IT, THERE JUST AREN'T ANY YALIES SO HARD UP THEY WANT TO GET INVOLVED WITH A NICE LOCAL GIRL...
HI, THERE! MY NAME'S MIKE!
LET ME QUALIFY THAT...
G B Trudeau

WELL, I GUESS IT'S ALRIGHT TO WALK WITH YOU FOR A BIT, MIKE. AFTER ALL YOU'RE A CELEBRITY AND YOU DON'T SEEM THAT BAD A SORT.
4-11
YUP, WELL HOW ABOUT'S WE GO ON UP TO THE ROOM AND HIT THE OLD HAY?
OH MY GOD! IT'S TRUE! YOU DO SAY THINGS LIKE THAT! HOW COULD YOU SAY THAT? WE JUST MET! WELL, I WON'T STAND FOR THAT! NO SIR! GOODBY TO YOU!
I'VE GOT TO WORK ON MY TIMING.
GBTrudeau

IT'S THE END OF AN EXHAUSTING REGISTRATION DAY AS PERT CO-ED CATHY DILLWORTHY ANXIOUSLY AWAITS HER NEW ROOMMATE.
6-19
ACTUALLY, I'M EXTREMELY UP FOR MEETING HER, AS I AM CONFIDENT SHE WILL BE A REAL WINNER.. AS PART OF YALE'S PROGRAM TO MATCH COMPATIBLE ROOMMATES, A SPECIAL ROOMING COMPUTER IS BEING USED.
KNOCK
KNOCK
HI THERE! GUESS WHAT! I'M YOUR NEW ROOMMATE! MY NAME'S MIKE "THE MAN" DOONESBURY AND MOST GIRLS ADORE ME! GLAD TO MEET YOU, ROOMIE!
OF COURSE, THERE ARE STILL A FEW BUGS IN THE SYSTEM...
GBTrudeau

EVEN THOUGH I NOW ENTER MY SECOND DAY OF SUSPENSION, I FEEL A TREMENDOUS SENSE OF RELIEF.
MY WHOLE BODY TELLS ME, "MEGAPHONE MARK, YOU SUSPENDED STUD, WHAT A SENSE OF RELIEF. NO MORE RESPONSIBILITIES AT ALL!"
FOR WITH SUSPENSION HAS COME FREEDOM! AT LAST I AM FREE FROM THE SHACKLES OF MY PAST. I AM MY OWN MAN. THE LAST TWO DAYS OF BEING FREE HAVE BEEN BLISS.... AH, A LETTER...
YALE STATION
"GREETINGS..."
YALE STATION
SO MUCH FOR MY PERIOD OF GRACE....
YALE STATION
GBTrudeau

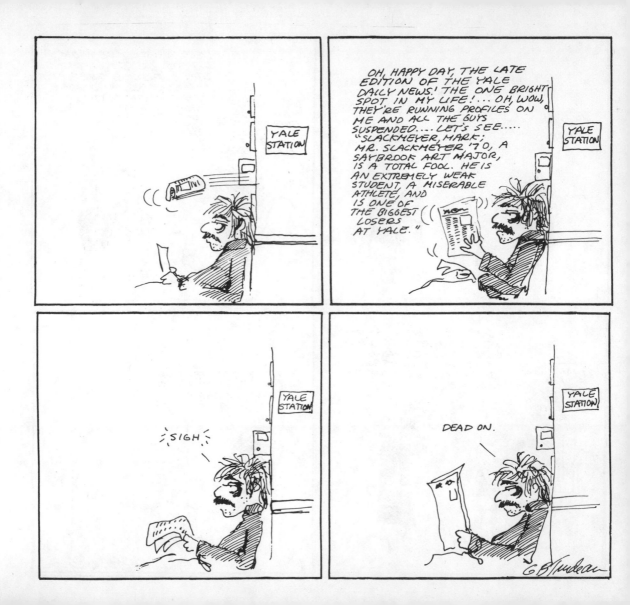

WELL, THIS MUST QUALIFY AS THE WORST DAY OF MY LIFE. YUP, HERE I AM WAITING FOR MY BLIND DATE AND I HAVE JUST BEEN TIPPED OFF THAT SHE MORE CLOSELY RESSEMBLES AN APE THAN A GIRL.
BUS STOP
THEN TO TOP THINGS OFF, I DISCOVER SHE IS THE SHORTEST GIRL AT HER COLLEGE. GREAT! JUST WHAT I NEED- AN UGLY MIDGET... OH, NO, HERE COMES THE BUS! WELL, CHIN UP, KIDDO!
BUS STOP
SAY! SHE DOESN'T APPEAR TO BE ON THE BUS! OH, HAPPY DAY, MY WEEKEND IS SAVED! WELL, GUESS I'LL BE GETTING BACK TO THE DORM NOW.
BUS STOP
BUS STOP
NOT SO FAST, BUSTER.
GBTrudeau

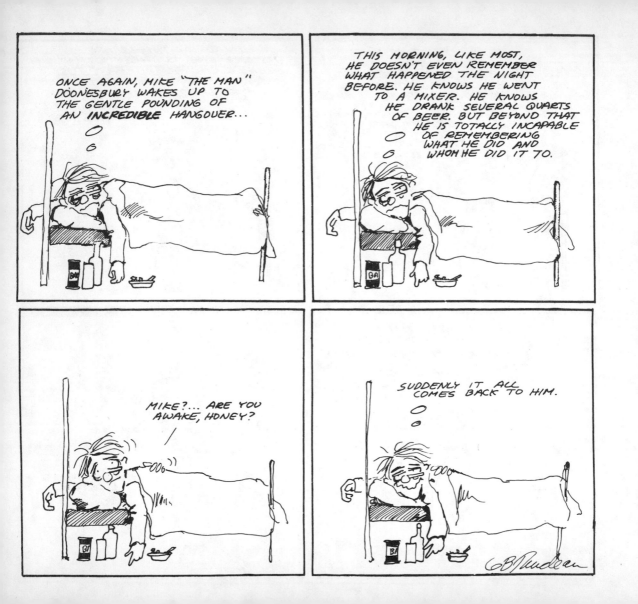

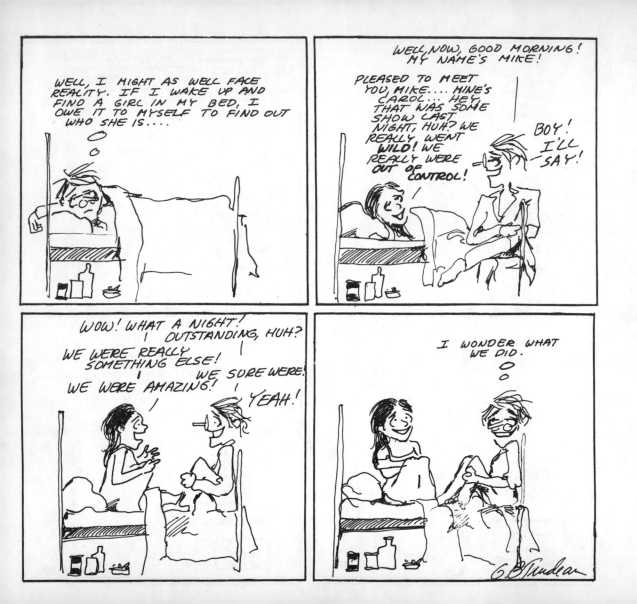

HERE I AM ONCE AGAIN AT THE STATION, WAITING FOR AN OLD FLAME, MILDRED, TO ARRIVE ON THE NOON BUS. BOY! TALK ABOUT EXCITEMENT.
BUS STOP
OL' MILLIE CERTAINLY WAS EXCITED WHEN I CALLED HER UP AND INVITED HER FOR A COLLEGE WEEKEND. I'LL BET SHE'D BEEN PINING AWAY FOR ME, CRYING HERSELF TO SLEEP, ALL THE WHILE THINKING, "MIKE, DEAR MIKE! HOW I LOVE THEE, MIKE!
RALPH!
STOP
RALPH! HOW ARE YOU, RALPH! HOW DIVINE TO SEE YOU AGAIN!
BUS STOP
NOT RALPH, EH? DICK. IT'S DICK, ISN'T IT? NO? HOW ABOUT BILL, WILLY? NO, DON'T TELL ME, IT'S NICK, RIGHT? NO...
BUS STOP
GBTrudeau

GARRY TRUDEAU, 26, grew up in Saranac Lake, New York. He attended Yale College, and later, Yale Art School, where he received a Master of Fine Arts degree in 1973. His comic strip "Doonesbury," which he started in college, is now syndicated in over 400 newspapers in the U.S. and abroad. Trudeau was awarded the Pulitzer Prize for Excellence in Journalism in 1975.

A resident of New Haven, Connecticut, Garry Trudeau is a fellow of Davenport College at Yale.